Through HIS EYES

Through HIS EYES

Rethinking What You Believe about Yourself

VIRGINIA H. PEARCE

M.

DESERET
BOOK

SALT LAKE CITY, UTAH

Library of Congress Cataloging-in-Publication Data

Pearce, Virginia H. author.
  Through His eyes : rethinking what you believe about yourself /
Virginia H. Pearce.
      p.   cm.
  Includes bibliographical references and index.
  ISBN 978-1-60641-242-8 (hardbound : alk. paper)
  1. Truth—Religious aspects—Christianity.   2. Church of Jesus Christ of Latter-day Saints—Doctrines.   3. Mormon Church—Doctrines.   4. Mormons—Conduct of life.
I. Title.
  BV4501.3.P434 2011
  248.4'89332—dc22   2011001629

Printed in the United States of America
Publishers Printing, Salt Lake City, UT

10   9   8   7   6   5   4   3   2   1

To my mother, father, and husband,
who loved Truth

CONTENTS

ACKNOWLEDGMENTS

B ecause the ideas in this book have developed over decades of time, I am indebted to many who cannot be remembered or named. Some of these fountains of information were found in scholarly works and in the front of classrooms. But many more were those patient enough to share, listen and respond as I tried to figure out, understand, assimilate, and modify my thinking. They have stimulated and inspired me.

A profound thanks to my friends at Deseret Book who have encouraged and provided opportunities for me to express the thoughts in this volume. Sheri Dew, Cathy Chamberlain, Jana Erickson, Emily Watts, Laurel Christensen, and the members of the editorial committee have been such remarkable mentors and friends. They have been particularly patient with my personal circumstances during the past two and a half years and yet unfailingly encouraging.

I wish to acknowledge those whose skills have created a pleasing and readable product out of a lot of 8½-by-11-inch pages of boring Times New Roman typeface. Sheryl Dickert, Richard Erickson, Tonya Facemyer, and Kayla Hackett, your decisions have interpreted and beautifully enhanced the message.

Most of all, I am thankful for the doctrines of The Church of Jesus Christ of Latter-day Saints—for Truth restored—and for the Holy Ghost who carries it into our hearts and minds.

Chapter One

THE CLOSET

*Don't own so much clutter that you
will be relieved to see your house catch fire.*

WENDELL BERRY

L ast week I cleaned out a closet. One closet, that's all. Still,
it took me years to get to it, one full day to completely
unload it, and more days than you would believe to disperse
the things that wanted to return to their old spots. There were
empty places on shelves and there was a kind of magnetic force
operating to get the "things" to leap up and back into their
familiar places. But I resisted. You see, I had a plan, and I was
determined to return to the closet only things that were useful
or had such great personal value that I *chose* to keep them. The
operative word here is *chose*.

I picked up each item as I took it from the closet. Then I

picked up each item again, thought about its use, and made a conscious decision—either returning it to a new spot in the closet or putting it in one of four piles on the floor. I designated one pile for the garbage, another for things to give away to family members or friends who might use them, a third for Deseret Industries, and the fourth for things I wanted to put in other spots in the house where they could be more readily used.

When those four piles were gone—days and days after the initial explosion of energy—I celebrated! And I felt very smart. You see, for many, many years I have failed to clean that way. I just didn't know that it would make such a big difference to pick up every single item—take every single thing out of the closet, room, or cupboard—thus forcing me to make a measured decision about what to put back in. Rather than take everything out, I would look at a cupboard or closet shelf by shelf, removing what I thought wouldn't serve me well. Then, when things got a bit roomier, I would move on. I failed to be thoughtful and thorough. Consequently, it was only a matter of months before I was back where I started—too much clutter in every given space.

Now, kind reader, you may be guffawing. I'm sure this is a principle you picked up a long time ago and are wondering why it took me decades to figure out. I'm certain there are books that told you this, or home organization lecturers, or mothers, sisters, or friends. But, if, like me, you didn't hear and hearken, just give it a try now. If you decide to deal with the clutter in a closet, begin by taking out *every single thing* and *thinking about it* before you put *anything* back in. It's just that simple. I warn you that this takes a bit longer than just removing a few items would, but the result is far more pleasing.

❧

Now come with me down a different road, because this book isn't about overloaded closets. It's actually a book about cluttered minds and hearts—ones that are full of glorious truths, but that are also home to a few too many troublesome things that are neither true nor useful. Yes, I'm talking about your mind and my mind.

I know of a missionary who noticed some of the clutter in his head. He reported that he got a new companion and, as they were riding their bikes along the first day, the elder was about twenty feet in front of him, right in his sight line. It was flat, boring pavement, and the new companion in front kept taking his hands off the handlebars and riding along with no hands. Our missionary observed this and then became aware of the thoughts in his own head: "I could never do that. He's a way better missionary than I am. This is going to be awful, working with someone who can do everything. It won't be long before he finds out what a failure I am. I can't do anything. I just wish this whole mission would be over . . ."

> *The sculptor produces the beautiful statue by chipping away such parts of the marble block as are not needed— it is a process of elimination.*
>
> ELBERT HUBBARD

That's a lot of clutter in one mind and heart. There is so much clutter, in fact, that our missionary friend can't get to the really valuable beliefs that are tucked in somewhere in the rubble, beliefs like, "I am a child of God with my own gifts and talents. My missionary companion is also a child of God with his own gifts and talents. When both of us bring those gifts to Him, He will magnify them so that we can both be good missionaries."

We all live with precious and true beliefs, but, not unlike our missionary friend, we also all have a certain amount of clutter that gets in our way. We have to be pretty brave to be willing to look inside and determine whether something is true or if it is just noisy and useless junk.

In what has become the first verse of Joseph Smith's history, he stated his desire to set down the facts of his life for public perusal. He described his audience—the people to whom his history was and is directed—as "inquirers after truth."

I like everything about that descriptive title: inquirer after truth. It seems to imply humility, courage, faith, an allegiance to straight thinking, a kind of mental toughness. I believe it is a description I would like to own myself—the kind of person I would like to be—and I suspect you feel the same.

In order to be inquirers after truth, you and I must be willing to embark with enthusiasm on a personal adventure. It is a journey outside as well as inside of ourselves. It is not the journey of an afternoon or a semester or a year. In essence, it requires the periodic exercise of taking everything out of the closet of our minds and purposefully returning only that which is truly useful—or actually true. Over and over again. Things that aren't true tend to creep into the great storage vaults of our minds, making it more difficult for us to see and use the great truths that belong there.

Inquiring after truth is a lifelong journey. Because there is

> *I have been induced to write this history, to disabuse the public mind, and put all inquirers after truth in possession of the facts, as they have transpired, in relation both to myself and the Church, so far as I have such facts in my possession.*
>
> JOSEPH SMITH—HISTORY 1:1

no end to truth, we will expect to continually see new truths or to understand old truths more fully and deeply. We will constantly be evaluating and integrating new truths, and evaluating and discarding partial truths and lies.

So, would you put that label on yourself, at least for a bit? Would you join me in acting as an energetic inquirer after truth—or a professional cleaner-outer-of-closets? Could we punch and probe, weigh and measure, explore and experiment together? Would you be willing to look deeply into your own mind and do a little reevaluating, discovering, sorting, sifting, discarding, and acquiring?

An orderly mind devoid of clutter and operating with useful truth is a good thing. Trust me, it will feel good. Very good.

Chapter Two

A USEFUL MAP

A road map always tells you
everything except how to refold it.

AUTHOR UNKNOWN

Our inquiring adventure will be easier to navigate if we are all looking at the same map. This map, of course, can't fully explain the very complex and individual ways we experience thoughts, emotions, and behavior, but it might help us to visualize a kind of sequential flow—even if it is grossly oversimplified.

The starting point for the journey we repeat over and over is the flow of outside information coming in through our five senses—in addition to that sixth sense, our spiritual sensations. We hear words, see and hear nonverbal messages, smell, touch and are touched by others, and sense spiritual promptings. In short, we take in all the data from the world outside of us.

This data has no real meaning until we sort and sift through it, interpreting it in terms of our past experience and the beliefs we already hold. And so, within seconds of our receiving the data, meaning is attached, resulting in an emotional response, which is followed by action of some sort. This is a road we travel countless times each day. Our subjective experience is that it is automatic—we hear or see something, and our emotions move us to respond. It just happens. And it happens quickly and almost continuously. Therefore, we might not even imagine that it is open to modification.

A quick example:

The starting point is **Data Input**: The counselor in Relief Society calls to ask me if I will teach Relief Society in two weeks.

I rapidly move the data through my filter of **Thoughts/Interpretations/Beliefs**: I am not a good teacher; she probably asked me because she feels sorry for me and wants me to feel important.

Within a nanosecond there is an **Emotional Response**: Fear, anxiety, embarrassment.

As these thoughts and emotions work in me throughout

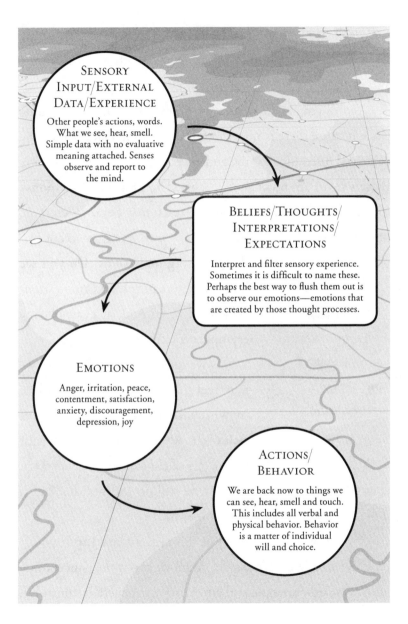

SENSORY
INPUT/EXTERNAL
DATA/EXPERIENCE

Other people's actions, words.
What we see, hear, smell.
Simple data with no evaluative
meaning attached. Senses
observe and report to
the mind.

BELIEFS/THOUGHTS/
INTERPRETATIONS/
EXPECTATIONS

Interpret and filter sensory experience.
Sometimes it is difficult to name these.
Perhaps the best way to flush them out is
to observe our emotions—emotions that
are created by those thought processes.

EMOTIONS

Anger, irritation, peace,
contentment, satisfaction,
anxiety, discouragement,
depression, joy

ACTIONS/
BEHAVIOR

We are back now to things we
can see, hear, smell and touch.
This includes all verbal and
physical behavior. Behavior
is a matter of individual
will and choice.

the week, they shape my **Behavior**: On Sunday I stumble through the lesson, communicating anxiety to everyone in the audience.

And of course, the road now doubles back in a continuing circle because there is now more **Information/Data Input** (the perceived discomfort of the audience) coming in to confirm my **Beliefs** that I am not a good teacher. The **Emotional Response** I have the next time I am asked to teach may be so much more uncomfortable that the **Action** I take is to refuse to accept further teaching invitations. Do you see how this automatic process grows stronger and stronger? And, in a case like my example here, more debilitating?

As we look at this progression, we may feel that the most sensible place in which to intervene is with our **Behavior**. After all, our own behavior is a matter of choice. So we try and try, making resolutions about what we will do and not do. And it sometimes works, but often it does not.

Should we try to stop all of this at the **Data Input** point? Probably not. We can't usually do much about the data coming in because other people and circumstances generally control it.

> *We are what we think.*
> *All that we are arises*
> *with our thoughts.*
> *With our thoughts,*
> *we make the world.*
>
> BUDDHA

So what about **Emotions?** Unfortunately, they seem to have a life of their own—we usually aren't very successful about simply making a decision not to be anxious. Emotions can be so strong and seem to come unbidden. What to do?

I am going to postulate that the **Beliefs/Thoughts/Interpretations/Expectations** seg-ment in this ongoing cycle is the most profoundly important. It is the driver of emotions and actions. It provides the filter through which we process all the sensory information in our envi-ronment. Furthermore, I am also go-ing to suggest that this "spot on the map" is fairly consistent over time and also the biggest mystery—both to our-selves and to others. Others cannot see what beliefs we are operating out of—and often we don't either. Our "Belief Boxes" hold a multitude of things—many of them deeply personal and specific to us as individuals. And we are what we think. Our emotions and our actions spring from our beliefs.

But this much I can tell you, that if ye do not watch yourselves, and your thoughts, and your words, and your deeds, . . . even unto the end of your lives, ye must perish. And now, O man, remember, and perish not.

MOSIAH 4:30

Joseph Smith wrote the thirteen Articles of Faith as state-ments of belief in his letter to John Wentworth. President

Gordon B. Hinckley, at a BYU devotional, referred to that as he shared with us ten statements of his personal beliefs in 1992. In that talk, President Hinckley said: "Each of us is largely the product of his or her beliefs. Our behavior is governed by these. They become our standards of conduct" ("I Believe," 2). Do you recognize the flow from our road map? *Our behavior grows out of our beliefs*. Yes. And along with our behavior come the emotions that motivate our behavior.

Will you, my friend, accept an invitation to inquire after truth as we poke around in our own individual Belief Boxes? What we have stored in there is important enough to spend some time and energy investigating.

Chapter Three

WE ALL BELIEVE—
SOMETHING

Every normal and accountable person believes something.
Such is a part of the natural heritage that goes with existence
itself. . . . The thought process is inherent in life itself and
we cannot exist without believing something.
ELDER BRUCE R. McCONKIE, *NEW WITNESS*, 22

L et's begin our journey at your Belief Box—a term we will use to describe the part of your mind that houses your thinking and believing. Pick up a pencil and begin to write. Begin each sentence with the words *I believe . . .* and just keep writing. Don't censor or organize. Just let it flow. You can list big, universal beliefs as well as small pieces of wisdom you hear yourself repeating from time to time. You'll have opportunities later to edit, add, delete, and reword—this is a first draft. Brainstorm. (In this case, that means storming into the brain and seeing what's there!) Just do some sightseeing. Write on the pages provided below or, if that is difficult for you, in your journal; or, if that is too much, just use a scrap of nonintimidating paper. Keep thinking and keep writing. Get as much on paper as you can. It may help you to think about the following:

- Beliefs I hold about God, the world, and how it all works.
- Beliefs I hold about people in general.
- Beliefs I hold about myself.

Think back on our closet-cleaning procedure. We are trying to take *everything* out of the closet. As we go forward, you will be able to take some time to consider each item and decide what you want to put back into your Belief Box as well as what is no longer useful to you. Focus and think beyond the obvious. Be brave. This is where you need to be a fearless inquirer after truth. There may be some information that you're not really proud of or that seems ridiculous. For instance, you may carry a belief that people in general are selfish and perhaps even out to get you. You may carry the belief that you are fat, along with the belief that fat people are not valued. Way in the back of your Belief Box, you may have carefully stored the thinking that if people really knew you they wouldn't love you. Along with those beliefs, you will be surprised to find conflicting beliefs existing right beside them—things such as your belief that you are loved by God, that He knows you completely and loves you completely. Just write everything down as it comes to mind, whether it makes sense or not.

Then, in the next chapter, we'll talk about how to sort through and organize the beliefs you've pulled out of your Belief Box.

Chapter Four

TRUE, TRUE, AND NOT-TRUE-AT-ALL

*Truth is truth, and it is
independent of whether it is believed or not.*

PRESIDENT BOYD K. PACKER, *MINE ERRAND*, 577

Now that we're inside our Belief Box, rummaging around, getting all confused, let's create three big piles so that we can do some separating out and organizing. These three piles—or compartments in the Belief Box—are based on Truth. They are:

1. Truth with a capital *T,*
2. truth with a lowercase *t,* and
3. beliefs that are not true at all. This is quite important, because not all of our beliefs are true. Some are actually lies.

When we clean out a closet, we examine the things we find on the basis of whether they are useful or whether they have some importance beyond useful-ness that would indicate a desire to keep them—some satisfying personal value.

Just because we think it or believe it doesn't mean it's true.

Similarly, we'll clean out the Belief Box on the basis of deciding which things in it are true, because only things that are true deserve to be in the precious recesses of our minds and hearts. In other words, we will be looking inside our box as inquirers after truth.

SORTING PILE #1: "TRUTHS"

First, there are **Truths.** Truth with a capital *T.* Core Truths or Absolute Truths. Independent Truths, true whether we believe them or not. Eternal Truths. Things that are true not only for this life, but for always. The criteria for determining whether a belief can be described as Truth are simple. The belief must pass a test:

1. Is it true eternally?
2. Is it true independent of whether people believe it or not?

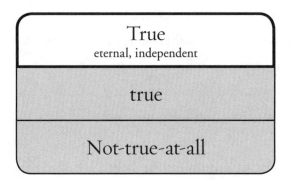

I'm sure you have some of these Truths on your list. They are what we readily think of when someone asks the question, especially in a Sunday School class: "What do you believe?"

Some of the Truths with a capital *T* that I carry in my Belief Box are:

- God the Father and His Son Jesus Christ live. They know me, they love me, and their work and glory is to bring about my growth and exaltation. I carry their spiritual DNA. The Atonement is evidence of their great love and allows me to hope for a great reunion with them.

- I exercise my agency and am accountable to God—first, last, and always—and I will not be here on earth forever.

- I am under covenant obligation to build His kingdom and to help my fellow beings return home to Him.

• I believe in the power of covenants—that as I keep my covenants, He is bound to never desert me.

Look at your list from the previous chapter—all of the items you identified as beliefs. Are there some that would qualify as Truths? Either put a capital *T* next to them or, if you really want to get tidy, copy them onto a separate piece of paper. There may be many more than my four (I could go on and on here) or perhaps one or two fewer. Most of us will share these beliefs. Think of them as bedrock statements of your testimony. As you say them out loud, they will make perfect sense and help you feel solid and grounded.

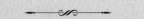

Truth is knowledge of things as they are, and as they were, and as they are to come.

D&C 93:24

SORTING PILE #2: "TRUTHS"

Inquiring further into our Belief Box, we find a second category of beliefs. These are a little bit harder to uncover. We generally don't think about them right off when someone asks us what we believe. Even so, you may have put some of them on your list. They are often things our mothers and fathers taught us that continue to resonate in our heads long after our parents are gone. Sometimes they come from our culture—church or family or ethnic. Most of the time they are good and useful truths. They often fall in the category of wisdom or good advice. Although they may rest to some degree on eternal Truths, in and of themselves they really have to do with this life and can't stand the way they are stated through eternity.

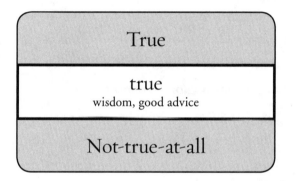

Very often we act out of these truths. Our inner ear often hears them as "shoulds." These beliefs can get a bit tricky when we use them to interpret and filter incoming data. They are usually more specific, narrow, and limiting than eternal Truths, and if we treat them as if they were eternal Truths, they can wreak havoc with our emotions and behavior.

For example, you may have this one in your head: "I believe that my home should be tidy and orderly before I go to bed at night." This is a very useful little belief and could have endless variations. You may have come to believe it because it was taught to you by your mother or by your own life experience. It's useful—and could be called true. But you can also see how it could get you and those who love you into a lot of trouble if you elevated it to Truth status. Then it becomes a supreme Truth, and you might put other things at risk in order to accomplish it—your health, your relationships, your ability to enjoy others.

On the other hand, when we examine this belief, we see that it does rest to some extent on eternal Truth. God is a God of order. Order is necessary for peace and eternal progression. The "shoulds" about housekeeping stay in place if we can remember to see them in the light of eternal Truth. In fact, housekeeping can turn from frustration to fulfillment with this sort of exercise.

More examples of some of the small-*t* "truths" I hold in my personal Belief Box might include the following:

- I believe I should make a contribution, be responsible, do my share of the work and a little bit more.
- I believe good relationships are my job.
- I believe that part of caring for my body is to be at

optimal weight—or a few pounds less. Furthermore, people who are thin are more acceptable to others.

• I believe if you plan well and work your plan, you can be successful.

I had my first baby at the age of twenty-two. My husband was in medical school and I took my last final exam for my own bachelor's degree the week after I brought my newborn daughter home from the hospital. The changes in my life were monumental. Suddenly, my varied and interesting life was confined to the geographic space of our two-bedroom apartment. It was just this inscrutable little baby and me—all day long, and some nights when her father was at the hospital. We lived in a city quite distant from my family and I knew very little about being a mother. I had no neighbors who were home during the day, so there was no adult conversation until Jim returned at night. There were, of course, things about my new life that I loved, but I found myself feeling more and more frustrated and discouraged. I thought that I was failing and didn't know how to succeed. You can imagine that the accompanying emotions were less than pleasant.

It slowly dawned on me, as I sought to understand my feelings, that I had some beliefs about success and how to achieve it that were working against me. One of those beliefs could be summed up in the familiar adage: "If you plan well and work your plan, you can be successful." I thought it was "True." It turns out that it is "true."

You see, operating on this belief, I planned more, worked even harder, and still this center of my world continued with her colic and fussy temperament. I became more and more discouraged. I would read another parenting book and pray every day to get better organized or to figure out a better plan. Slowly it dawned on me that I was praying for the wrong things. Finally, I asked the Lord to teach me how to enjoy and love my new life. And over time, that's what happened. Part of that came when I recognized I was using beliefs that had been useful in other areas of my life but produced only negative emotions when applied to mothering a newborn.

When I dug beneath the small truth, looking for eternal Truth, things began to fall into place. Some of the great underlying Truths that created peace and joy for me included the Truth that parenting is a partnership between God and mothers and fathers, and that when we turn our hearts and energies toward Him, He will consecrate our performance (no matter how lacking) to the welfare of our souls—and, I believe, to the souls of our children (see 2 Nephi 32:9).

Perhaps you would like to take a moment to look back at your list. Are there adages, bits of wisdom and advice your parents or teachers passed on to you, that usually work quite well but aren't really in the category of "Truth"? What about your beliefs about relationships? Look at your beliefs for a moment, then write what you know about relationships in an eternal sense—perhaps it would include the Truth that they go on forever and that we have a responsibility to help others back Home. But add the Truth that we each have agency. That is an eternal Truth. Are you understanding how this works? All "shoulds" have their roots in a Truth, but they are also tempered by other Truths.

On your list of beliefs, mark the small truths with a lower-case *t* or copy them onto a separate list. These messages from parents or culture are generally powerful. If you have identified some of them, look at them carefully and determine what "Truths" they rest on. State the eternal Truth next to them and see how it enlarges the belief. Notice the emotions that accompany that thinking. For me, there is always a slight relaxation and sense of peace that comes with putting my thinking into the context of the great plan of happiness.

SORTING PILE #3: "NOT-TRUE-AT-ALL"

Oddly enough, the last compartment in our Belief Box contains those things that aren't true at all. These are slippery little guys.

We are generally unaware that such ideas are in our Belief Box, because when we dig everything out and look at them, they don't make sense. In fact, they are laughable. Unfortunately, however, they can be very powerful in determining our emotions and our behavior. I doubt that you listed these among your beliefs. And yet, I think most of us have some of them operating to some degree or another.

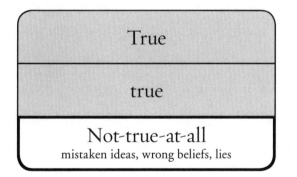

Examples might include the following:

- I believe I am a failure because not every relationship in my life is healthy and happy.

- I believe that if I don't come through 100 percent of the time, everyone will lose respect for me.
- I believe that God shows His pleasure and trust by the callings people receive. The more "important" the calling, the more He trusts and values you.
- When anything goes wrong in my marriage or family, it's always my fault. My children's failures are really my failures; my husband's rages are evidence of my stupidity in always making him mad.
- I believe that I don't really belong in Relief Society.

Perhaps the best way to flush these nontruths out of the closet—to even know they are *in* the closet—is to observe our emotions. Am I incredibly anxious and uptight? Am I filled with fear?

Let's talk about our emotions. Emotions reflect our beliefs and expectations. They do not initiate themselves, coming out of nowhere, as we sometimes think. Identifying our emotions can help us to look at other parts of our road map.

This is where we, as inquirers after truth, have to be willing to be a bit brave. As members of the true and living Church, we somehow think that if we act out of such stupidity, it must mean we don't have a testimony. That is another not-true-at-all

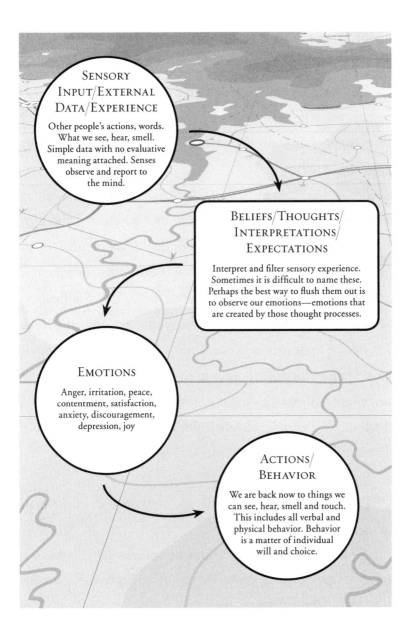

Sensory Input/External Data/Experience

Other people's actions, words. What we see, hear, smell. Simple data with no evaluative meaning attached. Senses observe and report to the mind.

Beliefs/Thoughts/Interpretations/Expectations

Interpret and filter sensory experience. Sometimes it is difficult to name these. Perhaps the best way to flush them out is to observe our emotions—emotions that are created by those thought processes.

Emotions

Anger, irritation, peace, contentment, satisfaction, anxiety, discouragement, depression, joy

Actions/Behavior

We are back now to things we can see, hear, smell and touch. This includes all verbal and physical behavior. Behavior is a matter of individual will and choice.

in our Belief Box—an idea that perhaps will become clearer in the following chapter.

But, back to our map. Notice the way the arrows flow. If there is an entry point in this cycle, it would be the Sensory Data Input. Emotions *do not start the process* in motion. They grow out of beliefs.

Most of us wrongly believe that there is nothing that can be done about emotions. They are what they are and we are helpless in their wake. Anger is a good example. We can dismiss it, but suddenly it pops up somewhere else—where we were not expecting it. After all, we feel what we feel. It's very difficult to be successful in simply ignoring or stuffing strong emotions. They come up somewhere else. Feelings also seem very complicated because they often occur in combination—we can be sad and angry at the same time, for instance.

But just because we feel it doesn't make it so, any more than our merely believing something means it is true.

So how do feelings shift or change?

Emotions shift dramatically when other parts of the map change.

We can change our thinking as we reassess and examine our beliefs for their validity. And when our thinking changes, our emotions will change automatically.

So, becoming an inquirer after truth is a pretty important occupation. No wonder we talk about the emotions of joy and peace and love as fruits of the Spirit (see Galatians 5:22). They follow Truth.

Chapter Five

GETTING PERSONAL

Confession is good for the soul only in the
sense that a tweed coat is good for dandruff—
it is a palliative rather than a remedy.

PETER DE VRIES

This chapter is required reading only if you are confused about how this all works in real life. I apologize for being personal, but mine is the only mind that I have exclusive rights to publish!

Not too many years ago, I was scheduled to participate in a Deseret Book–sponsored Time Out for Women event in Calgary, Canada. Because it would fall on our anniversary, my husband and I thought that it would be pleasant for us to go together, rent a car following the conference, and spend a few days vacationing in the Canadian Rockies. We planned to fly to Calgary on a Friday morning; I would participate in the conference on Friday night and again on Saturday; then we would go our merry way.

About 6:00 P.M. on Thursday evening, when we should have been packing, I noticed that the peaches on our tree were suddenly and completely ripe, so we began bottling them when Jim got home from work. We were elbow deep in peach peelings and sticky syrup when I asked him about his passport. "Are you sure it's not expired? You know that you have to have a passport now to fly into Canada?" Even as I said it, I had a sinking feeling. He responded that he hadn't used his passport in quite a while and he had no idea what the expiration date was.

His hands were sticky so I went to look, taking the stairs two at a time. Whew. His passport was just fine. Then I looked at mine, only to discover that it had expired the month before!

Now, here's where things got crazy. I truly hit a panic button. My anxiety level went into overdrive and I couldn't think well enough to even have a conversation with Jim, let alone think clearly about alternatives. It was, of course, after hours for every government office there ever was, so I got on the Internet. To be sure, there are lots of services that can expedite a passport—for hundreds of dollars—which in my demented state I was perfectly willing to pay! I scrolled through each site but couldn't find one that could do it in ten hours' time. In retrospect, that was a miraculous blessing for our bank account, because at that moment of craziness I would have paid anything!

On the verge of tears, I stumbled back into the kitchen with what seemed to me an insolvable tragedy. Jim suggested that I call the Deseret Book folks who were already in Canada. I refused. It seemed just too humiliating. "Well, what's the alternative?" Jim responded. Since I couldn't think of one, I reluctantly agreed and made the call. I stumbled all over myself explaining my problem. We did some back-and-forthing with some on-site Canadians who thought that crossing the border in a car was a possibility, since the passport requirement was still new and there might be a grace period.

So, the next morning Jim and I got in the car and drove to Canada. Much to my surprise, the border guard was casual and nice and perfectly willing to accept my birth certificate, even though I was still eaten up with anxiety. We were in Calgary in time to participate in the Saturday meetings if not the Friday night one, where another presenter did my duties as host. So, it was certainly no loss for the audience (actually a gain) and no loss for the meeting planners. I couldn't help but sit down and think a bit when it was over. The puzzle in the whole episode was my out-of-control emotional state when I discovered what had happened. It was a kind of anxiety that had been out of the ordinary and completely debilitating.

As an inquirer after truth, let me share with you some of the beliefs that were present—beliefs that produced my spiraling emotions: "I am irresponsible." "I never seem to be able to keep all of the balls in the air." "I forget everything." "I never think ahead." "No one at Deseret Book will ever trust me to come through again."

Even as I write those beliefs down, it is obvious to me that they are not true. However, my emotions told me that those were the beliefs that I was acting out of.

I believe there were also some "truths" that were operating. These were bits of wisdom that came from my parents and were reinforced by others: "I should be willing to make a contribution. I should think ahead and do what I say I will do." These are true, but somehow I had them elevated to big Truths. In fact, when I stated the underlying eternal Truths, I felt an immediate decrease in my anxieties. I think that the Truths in this scenario could include the following: "I am under covenant obligation to help build His kingdom. As I seek to do that, I will make mistakes and will need to seek the forgiveness of others, the Lord, and myself. Furthermore, the success of the entire kingdom does not rest on my shoulders. I am only there to help Him."

Emotions are a gift of mortal life. We certainly don't want to intimate that we would want to be emotion free. Sadness, joy, sorrow, affection, love, peace, contentment, and even disappointment are driven by big Truths. But emotions become debilitating and pathologic when they are driven by (1) lies posing as truth, or (2) small truths unsupported by big Truths.

Now, just to make sure you know how to sort those beliefs that are running around in your head, try practicing on the following exercise:

Mark each statement below with a capital *T*, a lowercase *t*, or an *L*.

—— If people really knew me, they wouldn't love me.

—— Thin people are healthier and more pleasing to others.

—— We all make mistakes.

—— There is a right way and a wrong way to do everything.

—— You can't be too thin or too rich.

—— This life is not the end of our growth and progression.

—— People who keep the commandments are protected against trouble and heartache.

—— My body is a gift from God.

—— Although service is never convenient, it is something we should always be engaged in. Furthermore, the more service you perform, the more God and other people love you.

If you have questions on any of these, just mark the page and come back to it after you have read a few more chapters. We haven't provided an answer key—for very important reasons. This sorting and sifting is personal and a bit messy. But you'll get very good at it with practice.

As you read along, take time to go back to your belief list from chapter 3. Keep adding to it and do some sorting

Verily, verily, I say unto thee, blessed art thou for what thou hast done; for thou hast inquired of me, and behold, as often as thou hast inquired thou hast received instruction of my Spirit. If it had not been so, thou wouldst not have come to the place where thou art at this time.

D&C 6:14

as you desire. The most important thing you can do is to simply observe yourself. Listen to the chatter in your head. Don't talk back or make any judgments. Just listen. Slip into your "observing self" as you become aware of strong emotions—positive or negative—and try to hear the chatter that created the emotions. Don't do anything about it yet. Just watch and let it be. It's pretty interesting. Much more entertaining than watching reality television!

Expect to become more aware of the Spirit operating in your life. That's what happens when you are an honest inquirer after truth.

Chapter Six

FINDING AND STARVING THE HALF-TRUTHS AND LIES

Charlie Brown: "Sometimes I lie awake at night,
and ask, 'Where have I gone wrong?' Then a voice says to me,
'This is going to take more than one night.'"

CHARLES M. SCHULZ

In our limiting mortal state, none of us will probably ever be able to rid our minds and hearts of all of the half-truths and not-true-at-alls we carry around, but it seems reasonable that we would want to do everything we can to find them and starve them. If we don't know what they are, it's very easy for us to keep feeding them, helping them to grow more powerful and stronger by the day.

Hopefully, you have been observing your thoughts—that constant commentary in your head. Our inquiring job in the next two chapters is to identify, confront, and change the less-than-helpful beliefs we hold—those that are half-truths or out-and-out lies.

IDENTIFY

Out-of-whack emotions are always a good beginning point for identifying beliefs that aren't really true, an easy red flag for our inquiry. Exaggerated emotions of anxiety or discouragement invite us to trace them back to the thoughts that are creating them.

Remember the discouraged missionary in chapter 1? It was obvious to him that something was wrong because he was having difficulty getting out of bed in the morning and didn't want to talk to anyone. He was so depressed that he wanted to go home. Those kinds of emotions are a strong signal, letting us know that some investigation is in order.

In identifying where the trouble is coming from, the next step is to listen, to see if the chatter in your head contains all-or-nothing statements—never or always—especially negative statements about yourself. Try to articulate the belief; write it down where you can see it. Say it out loud.

Our missionary began listening to the chatter in his head. He noticed that there were many "never" and "always" statements, such as, "I could *never* do that." "This is going to be awful working with someone who can do *everything.*" "I can't do *anything.*" Furthermore, all the statements about himself were negative: "He's a way better missionary than I am." "It won't be long before he finds out what a failure I am."

Confront with Logic

In identifying the problem, try to articulate the underlying belief. Write it down. If you do this habitually, you will probably come up with two or three recurring beliefs about yourself or the world. Test them by saying them out loud. Our missionary found that one of the beliefs he was operating out of was "I am a complete failure." As he said that over and over again out loud, inviting it onto the center stage of his mind, it began to sound less and less logical. After all, he began to think of times when he *had* been successful. He began to think more clearly—to understand that there were many times when he had failed in his life, but just as many times when he had overcome failures or even times when he had done extremely well.

Elder M. Russell Ballard said:

> In my office hangs a printed statement that includes the last words spoken by my grandfather Elder Melvin J. Ballard before his passing. He was in the hospital phasing in and out of a coma. My father said that Grandfather suddenly opened his eyes and looked into the room and said, "Above all else, brethren, let us think straight." A few minutes later he passed away.
>
> That was more than 65 years ago. How much more does the world need people today who can think straight? ("Becoming Self-Reliant," 54).

Straight thinking demands discipline. You have to listen carefully and accurately—not only to what you hear others say, but to what you hear yourself say.

The Lord admonished Oliver Cowdery, "Study it out in your mind" (D&C 9:8). Paul wrote to Timothy, "For God hath not given us the spirit of fear; but of power, and of love, and of *a sound mind*" (2 Timothy 1:7; emphasis added).

If there are messages in your head about being a failure, or being irresponsible, define those terms. What exactly do you mean by *failure* or by *irresponsible?* Write down your definitions.

Be rigorous. As you struggle to find just the right words to describe what you mean by a given term, you will discover what you don't know right now. That's the magic of writing.

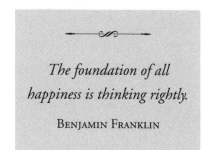

The foundation of all happiness is thinking rightly.

BENJAMIN FRANKLIN

Caution: Make sure that when you apply the standards for success or responsibility, they are ones that apply to others as well as yourself. That's the logical way. Remember, if your Belief Box is filled with standards for yourself that you never apply to others, you might be operating out of things that just aren't True!

EXAMINE THE EVIDENCE

As you begin to think straight, you'll want to examine the evidence, the experiences that created and continue to support your illogical beliefs. If they don't make sense, for heaven's sake, where *did* they come from?

I had an interesting—actually heartbreaking—conversation with a woman some years ago. She was a new acquaintance who had offered to drive me to the airport after a speaking engagement. We were talking about her interesting work, her family, just the things you talk about to become acquainted, when she surprised me by saying, "I feel so bad that the Lord doesn't trust me."

"What?" I said.

"Just that," she said. "He doesn't trust me."

"Really?" I responded. "How do you know that?"

"Well," she replied, "I've never been in a presidency."

We had only a moment to talk, but I have thought of that woman more than once. Surely the Lord shows His trust in us as we receive callings. But to limit Him so narrowly doesn't seem logical to me. This dear sister had served in many positions in the Church. She had just finished telling me about her profession. She worked in the medical field and had indicated that she had a special ability to comfort those who were struggling, even dying. It seems to me that being able to help others in that particular way is clear evidence of God's trust. It seems to me that teaching fifteen-year-old girls in Young Women, or giving children their first exposure to the Church in nursery, or being a visiting teacher to someone who is needing a lift, are all evidences of His trust. What about being worthy to receive the promises of the temple? Are those not evidences?

Somewhere there must have been some data coming in that made that woman form a belief that being in a presidency was very important. It must have been so powerful that it allowed her to filter out any data that might indicate differently.

I sometimes feel a little sad when we talk about someone's

continued faithfulness—gospel success—by saying, "And now he is a bishop," or a stake president, or a stake Relief Society president. I guess we are using that for a short way of saying, "He or she continues to grow and serve and keep covenants." But are we unwittingly sending messages that can contribute to illogical and damaging beliefs that God only expresses His approval by calling people to positions that are seen as having higher or lower value in a hierarchical sense?

As you look for evidences for your beliefs, try to be objective. Imagine that you are standing on a balcony, looking down on you and your life. Describe to a stranger what it looks like. And remember, this is all about "thinking straight."

I was discussing these ideas one day with a friend and she said, "Wait a minute. I've got a great example for you." She said that not too long ago she had heard a woman whistling. It was a happy sound, but it kind of startled her because she had a belief in her head that "girls don't whistle." This fifty-ish woman laughed, realizing that her mother had told her that when she was very young and somehow it had lodged in her brain and all these years she had simply never whistled. Well, when this belief popped up, along with the data that had created it, it was easy to see it for what it was—her mother's preference, but certainly not a commandment. She reported that she immediately started to whistle, just wanting to test it for herself, and found that it was a delightfully cheerful thing to do! And she didn't really feel less of a woman. Not a big deal, but kind of fun.

If there is a "should" statement like that in your head, challenge it. Ask some questions:

- Where did this rule come from?
- Does this rule apply to everyone, or just me? (Good "should" statements apply to everyone.)
- Is this rule a preference or a tenet?
- Have I tested this belief out for myself?

A woman named Angela Cummings, who joined the Church as an adult, tells this story:

> When I was younger, I tried out for glee club. My sister, who is a pretty good singer, looked at me and said, "Don't ever sing. You're off-key." I was at a delicate age, and I never opened my mouth to sing again. But as soon as I was baptized, I don't know what happened, but I was able to sing. It's the strangest thing, I was no longer afraid of being off-key. It's not that I have a great voice, but

singing suddenly became a pleasure in my life again (Kimball and Miles, *Mormon Women*, 31).

What do you suppose happened to Angela? We see in her, I believe, the Holy Ghost as a source of sensory data. Do not underestimate this. Spiritual sensory data is as real as seeing or touching. The Holy Ghost provides us with spiritual experiences—new data—that, if we allow it, will change the beliefs that help us filter and interpret all of the other data. It is *spiritual* data or *spiritual* experience, just as real as all of the other sensory data. We can either filter it out or use it to create and build Truth into our minds and hearts.

As you examine the data coming in, be rigorous. Are you ignoring some? Are you imagining some? Are you denying some? How are you interpreting or filtering the data to make it match what you are looking for in order to verify the beliefs you already hold?

A young woman was asked by a friend to stand on the curb of a busy street for five minutes and count the number of Toyotas that drove past. When she returned, prepared to report the number, she was instead asked how many Subarus she saw. She, of course, hadn't seen any. She was too busy looking for the Toyotas. We see or experience what we expect to see. Our preconceived beliefs actually determine what we experience.

Some of the not-true-at-all beliefs we hold are so powerful that we simply don't "see" or allow in any data that doesn't support them. We ignore conflicting experiences and give extra weight to those experiences that confirm the erroneous beliefs we have come to cherish—even while they cause pain and unhappiness.

As you think about experiences of the past that created a negative belief, seek to identify the experiences that support it *now*. Try to be objective. You may need someone to help you check it out—not defend or support it, just honestly check it out.

I know a woman who didn't like going to church. She said that week after week no one spoke to her, which confirmed her belief that she just didn't belong there. She decided to try to be more objective about her experience. This is what she explained to me:

> During the closing song I noticed that I packed up the diaper bag, the books, papers—everything, so that the minute the prayer was finished I could hurry out. Last Sunday, I noticed that as I leaned

down to pick up the diaper bag someone was coming up the aisle and was looking at me like she wanted to say something. More quickly than you could believe, I dove down into the diaper bag until she passed, grabbed the baby, and hurried out the other door. I guess I'm kind of making sure that all my experiences match my negative beliefs—even though I'm miserable! In fact, the idea of allowing myself to have other kinds of experiences scares me to death!

COSTS OR BENEFITS OF HOLDING THIS BELIEF

Ask yourself some hard questions. Things such as:

- Is this belief serviceable enough to hold onto?
- What does it get me? (For example, if you believe yourself to be a victim, there are protectors who might rally around you. Remaining a victim allows you to avoid the hard work of changing. It is predictable.)
- What does it cost me? (Staying the victim, however, might wear people out and keep you from the joy of helping and serving others.)

- What emotions would I feel, what would I do, if I held another belief?
- Does it "abound"? Do I feel like I am shriveling up inside or does my spirit abound? What are its fruits? Paul tells us that the fruit of the Spirit—that is, the fruit of holding true beliefs—is "love, joy, peace, longsuffering, gentleness, goodness, faith. . . . If we live in the Spirit, let us also walk in the Spirit" (Galatians 5:22, 25). Living in the Spirit means living out of Truth, not out of erroneous beliefs.

Watch for the beliefs expressed in the following passage by Richard Wright. Notice the experiences that created the beliefs. Look for the very real costs and benefits of continuing to hold each belief.

> My mother's suffering grew into a symbol in my mind, gathering to itself all the poverty, the ignorance, the helplessness; the painful, baffling, hunger-ridden days and hours; the restless moving, the futile seeking, the uncertainty, the fear, the dread; the meaningless pain and the endless suffering. Her life set the emotional tone of my life, colored the men and women I was to meet in the

future, conditioned my relation to events that had not yet happened, determined my attitude to situations and circumstances I had yet to face. A somberness of spirit that I was never to lose settled over me during the slow years of my mother's unrelieved suffering, a somberness that was to make me stand apart and look upon excessive joy with suspicion, that was to make me self-conscious, that was to make me keep forever on the move, as though to escape a nameless fate seeking to overtake me. . . .

At the age of twelve I had an attitude toward life that was to endure, that was to make me seek those areas of living that would keep it alive. . . . The spirit I had caught gave me insight into the sufferings of others, made me gravitate toward those whose feelings were like my own, made me sit for hours while others told me of their lives. . . .

It made me want to drive coldly to the heart of every question and lay it open to the core of suffering I knew I would find there (*Black Boy*, 100–101).

The experiences of Richard Wright's childhood put in place for him certain beliefs about life. The personal cost of carrying those beliefs was high. He lists some of the costs: "a somberness" of spirit, a suspicion of joy, self-consciousness, and a need to be constantly on the move. But he also names two benefits: insight into the suffering of others and a desire to hear of their lives. In his adult life as a writer, those benefits would enhance the understanding of thousands who would read his classic book, *Black Boy*. Only Wright would be able to decide if the benefits outweighed the costs, but he could do that only as he consciously examined the liabilities himself.

Similarly, as we examine the beliefs we find in our Belief Box, we will understand more clearly those that have benefited us and those that have made us unnecessarily unhappy. Great joy can come as we identify and discard the beliefs we have been carrying that are not true and do not serve us well.

Chapter Seven

FINDING HALF-TRUTHS AND LIES THROUGH QUESTIONS

Questions can motivate us to change because
they invite us to reflect. . . . If you want to change
your life, change your questions.

WENDY WATSON NELSON, *CHANGE YOUR QUESTIONS*, 6, 12

The questions in this chapter will continue to help you identify beliefs that fall in our third "sorting pile": half-truths and thoughts that just aren't true at all. These questions are simple, but they will be powerful if you will let them lead you into honest reflection. Don't justify your thinking; just identify it as you ask yourself the questions.

WHOSE MISSION DOES THIS BELIEF
SUPPORT—CHRIST'S OR SATAN'S?

Think about your belief in terms of the Savior or Lucifer. Whose mission does it support? Does your belief that you don't belong in Relief Society support the Savior's mission, or is that just what Satan would want you to believe? What about your belief that you have to succeed entirely on your own, that if people really knew you they wouldn't love you? Isn't that just what Satan would want you to believe? He wants us to feel "less than," to feel shameful and unworthy, to feel like we're on our own.

Elder Joseph B. Wirthlin taught us: "Some are lost because they are different. They feel as though they don't belong. Perhaps because they are different, they find themselves slipping away from the flock. They may look, act, think, and speak differently than those around them and that sometimes causes them to assume they don't fit in. They conclude that they are not needed. Tied to this misconception is *the erroneous belief that all members of the Church should look, talk, and be alike*" ("Concern for the One," 18; emphasis added).

Do you notice how erroneous beliefs cluster together? The belief that you are completely different from everyone else leads to the belief that you are not needed and is confirmed by the belief that everyone should look, talk, and be alike.

Satan is the father of lies, while Christ is the father of truth.

IS THERE DOCTRINE THAT WOULD BE PERTINENT TO UNDERSTANDING THE TRUTH OR FALSEHOOD OF THIS BELIEF?

Think of some of the basic doctrinal Truths that you know—the ones you listed in chapter 3 as well as those you hear taught in church, through the scriptures, and from the mouths of living prophets. Put those doctrines (unchanging and eternal) alongside the belief in question. Do they complement one another or are they mutually exclusive?

A basic doctrine of the Church of Jesus Christ is that we are the offspring of God, that He knows us completely and loves us with a perfect love. Is that doctrine pertinent in understanding whether some of your beliefs are True?

An example comes from the scriptures as Paul addresses the erroneous belief that money is everything, the "perverse disputings of men of corrupt minds, and *destitute of the truth,* supposing that gain is godliness . . . but godliness with contentment is great gain. For we brought nothing into this world, and it is certain we can carry nothing out. And having food and raiment let us be therewith content" (1 Timothy 6:5–8; emphasis added). Notice how he calls the belief that gain is godliness "destitute of the truth." And then he teaches the gospel truth that "godliness with contentment is great gain."

Another example: A doctrinal understanding of the Fall allows us to see that as mortals we are weak and will make mistakes. But because of the redemptive power of Jesus Christ, we can repent and go forward. Does this match the belief that making a mistake disqualifies me permanently from the love of others as well as that of God?

Elder Dallin H. Oaks clearly taught us to use our knowledge of truth (our testimonies) as a way to interpret our experiences. "Those who have a testimony of the gospel of Jesus Christ should interpret their experiences in terms of their knowledge of the purpose of life, the mission of our Savior, and the eternal destiny of the children of God" (*Pure in Heart,* 113).

CAN I ASK THE LORD?

Consider praying about things that you may not have prayed about before. Pray about a belief that is causing you pain. Ask Him if it is true. Trust Him. "Yea, Lord, I know that thou speakest the truth, for thou art a God of truth, and canst not lie" (Ether 3:12).

Moroni 10:4 is a familiar scripture: "And when ye shall receive these things, I would exhort you that ye would ask God, the Eternal Father, in the name of Christ, if these things are not true; and if ye shall ask with a sincere heart, with real intent, having faith in Christ, he will manifest the truth of it unto you, by the power of the Holy Ghost."

We usually interpret this verse to mean that if you read the Book of Mormon and pray in faith about it, He will let you know of its authenticity. Of course, it does mean that. Many of us have had that wonderful confirmation of the Truth of the Book of Mormon. However, the verse that follows is of great interest. It reads: "And by the power of the Holy Ghost ye may know the truth of all things" (v. 5). The truth of ALL things. We can pray and receive the witness of the Holy Ghost about the truth of *all* things.

When you pull a belief out of the closet—one that is precipitating troublesome emotions—pray about it, asking your Father in Heaven to show you the truth.

Are There Any Commandments Involved Here?

Nothing distorts our ability to discern truth of any kind more than failing to keep the commandments. Once we begin breaking commandments, we feel guilt and a certain amount of discomfort. It is an easy thing to simply rationalize away the belief—the commandment—thereby absolving ourselves of the need to repent and change and alleviating the immediate discomfort. It seems easy, but in the long run, it is never effective. Remember, beliefs precipitate emotions. But the emotion of guilt or godly sorrow that follows sin is meant to encourage us to repent—not to change our beliefs. In other words, when we start digging around in our Belief Box, if we throw out Truth, what we have left will *never, ever* bring us peace and happiness.

> *Behold, I say unto you, that they desire to know the truth in part, but not all, for they are not right before me and must needs repent.*
>
> D&C 49:2

Furthermore, the Holy Ghost is the revealer of Truth, and He is most able to operate in us when we are keeping the commandments. So losing the Holy Ghost makes our quest for Truth rather hopeless. That doesn't mean we have to be perfect to enjoy the companionship of the Holy Ghost. It means our desires and our actions must indicate that we believe in Him and love Him.

The word *repentance* comes from the Greek word *metanoia*. *Meta* is the Greek stem meaning "change." *Noia* means "thought" or "mind." So when we repent, it is a changing of our thoughts—our minds. In the words of the Bible Dictionary, it is "a fresh view about God, about oneself, and about the world" (s.v. "Repentance," 760). In the language we have been using, it is replacing erroneous beliefs with a mind filled with light and truth. Repentance is an ongoing process and will always be part of our mortal lives as inquirers after truth.

CAN I MAKE A DECISION ABOUT WHAT I WILL AND WILL NOT BELIEVE?

Use your agency. The story of Lamoni's father, the Lamanite king, and his willingness to give away all his sins to know God is touching to me (see Alma 22:18). This is an act of will, a choice we can make. Am I willing to give away my cherished little beliefs—even though they are somewhat comforting (in a perverse way) because of their familiarity? For instance, if I carry the belief that I am hopelessly inadequate and doomed to fail, I no longer feel that I must work diligently—so there is justification in not trying to do difficult things. For some people, that is an unhappy but comfortable way to live.

Don't be a helpless victim about this. You can make a decision about what you will choose to believe and what you will choose to let go of.

Elder Dallin H. Oaks gives good advice: "We all seem to have susceptibilities to one disorder or another, but whatever our susceptibilities, we have the will and the power to control our thoughts and our actions. This must be so. God has said that he holds us accountable for what we do and what we think, so our thoughts and actions must be controllable by our agency" (in Dollahite, ed., *Strengthening Our Families,* 224).

WHAT NEW EXPERIENCES WOULD I NEED IN ORDER TO CHANGE MY ERRONEOUS BELIEF?

Don't wait for experiences to just happen. We can actually create new experiences for ourselves. The friend described earlier, who discovered that she was actually helping to create the painful experience of not belonging at church, can make a decision. She can choose to speak to two or three people every Sunday. She can choose to initiate these conversations. She can choose to find things that she has in common with other ward members. She can choose to respond when others approach her—to look at them and smile. At first these new behaviors will be awkward, but as she persists, they will become more comfortable—and new sensory data will start to come. Ward members will begin to respond to her and be more free to initiate conversation when they are welcomed with a smile.

Of course, she must be careful not to filter the new data out by saying things like, "Well, they just smiled at me because I smiled at them—not because they like me." This isn't easy work when our filtering and interpreting habits are entrenched, but if our desires to live out of Truth, rather than out of lies, are great enough, we will persist.

All of us carry around troublesome little pockets of small truths or lies that cause us pain. Some of them can be easily dismissed once we recognize them. However, sometimes they are so deeply embedded that we need professional support to identify and change them. There is no shame in that. In our modern society we have doctors and lawyers to help us through illnesses or problems that we lack the skills to negotiate on our own. It is the same with therapists. If your emotions are chronically debilitating, you will want to consider getting good professional help.

I love the description of the brethren in the land of Zion (Missouri), "many of whom are truly humble and are seeking diligently to learn wisdom and to find truth. Verily, verily I say unto you, blessed are such, for they shall obtain; for I, the Lord, show mercy unto all the meek" (D&C 97:1–2).

Meekness and humility are required of inquirers after

truth. If we are diligent in our quest, the Lord will show us mercy, "for [we] shall obtain."

Do you remember the missionary we talked about in the first chapter? He was riding down the street behind his new companion when the elder in front took his hands off the handlebars. As our missionary observed the chatter in his own head, it included the following beliefs: "I could never do that. He's a way better missionary than I am. This is going to be awful, working with someone who can do everything. It won't be long before he finds out what a failure I am. I can't do anything. I just wish this whole mission would be over . . ."

As the elder observed his beliefs in the clear light of rational thought, they seemed a bit overdone. Could it be that he really believed things with so little logic? After all, what connection would there be between riding a bicycle without your hands and being a good missionary? As he continued to think about this little conundrum, he saw that there were some costs to his belief—the greatest being his own satisfaction and happiness. He had to admit that his beliefs were making him miserable. But—and this took some courage to admit—there were also some benefits. As long as he saw himself as a victim of his own inadequacies, he didn't really have to work hard. If he was a failure from the start, it would be futile to waste any energy; he could just be lazy, and perhaps they would send him home.

Furthermore, it was easy to see that holding those beliefs certainly supported Lucifer's agenda, not the Savior's. The Lord would want our missionary to value his companion, but He would also want our missionary to value himself and to take joy in a unified companionship—a much more effective way to teach the gospel. Lucifer wins, in his own twisted way, with every discouraged and unhappy missionary.

Our elder decided to take his beliefs to the Lord in prayer—that very night and every morning and night thereafter. He soon found that it was difficult to even ask the Lord to tell him if he was indeed a failure—it sounded like a ridiculous question. And so he began to ask the Lord to help him know that He was there and could help him become a good missionary. He wanted to know if that, indeed, was the Truth. In the midst of those personal, heartfelt prayers, our missionary decided to use his agency—to make a choice. He decided to give away his erroneous beliefs about himself and to accept the Truth, taught him by the Holy Ghost, that God loved him and would help him to succeed. In very small and gradual ways, things began to change.

Oh, and by the way, it wasn't long before he could be seen riding his bicycle down the street with a big grin on his face and his hands in the air!

Chapter Eight

FINDING AND FEEDING TRUTH

Then say, what is truth?
'Tis the last and the first,
For the limits of time it steps o'er.
Tho the heavens depart and the earth's fountains burst,
Truth, the sum of existence, will weather the worst,
Eternal, unchanged, evermore.

"OH SAY, WHAT IS TRUTH?" *HYMNS,* NO. 272

We have been working hard on the negative end so far—the pile containing those beliefs that don't deserve to be part of our Belief Box. We've been pulling out the weeds. Now let's do the fun part: planting, finding, tending, feeding, and enjoying the flowers. Our goal is to make the things that are really True in our Belief Box so healthy that they will literally crowd out, suffocate, and strangle those debilitating pockets of lies and half-truths. Perhaps we will understand in an even clearer way how valuable, how useful, and how satisfying Truth can become in our lives.

Several years ago I went on a river trip with my husband and some of our adult children. It was a brand-new experience, full of lots of excitement and great times in beautiful country. I also learned some things about myself—some things that surprised and confused me. Somehow, in the midst of one of the rapids, I was pitched out of the raft. It wasn't too scary and I was able to make my way back quickly. The surprise happened when I went to hoist myself up on the side of the raft so that I could get back in. Hmmm. I put my hands on the side and went to give myself an inner boost and nothing happened. After I had repeated the failed attempt two more times, those on board took pity on me and literally dragged me over the inflated side of the raft. Rather like a beached whale being dragged to safety. It was not a pretty sight, I'm sure, and I felt less than lovely. I thought about it a little bit, wondering where and how I had lost so much strength. Then, of course, we came back from the river trip and I went back to my life— not thinking too much about it.

But a couple of years later I had another "incident." I was on a small stepladder in my study dusting the highest shelves. Disturbing the delicate balance of the ladder, I reached a bit farther than I should have and the ladder began to tip toward the corner of the room, just a couple of feet away. I remember reaching for those core muscles again—the same ones that had failed me on the river trip—to bring myself and the ladder back into balance. And there was nothing there—again. The ladder and I just kept going for the wall. Total injuries were just bruises, albeit big and painful ones. Remembering my failed attempt to board the raft as well as the sudden grab for muscles that weren't there, I had cause to think seriously about my core muscles, or lack thereof.

It's obvious what needs to be done to develop core physical strength: consistent exercise (pushing just a little beyond your capacity)—forever. But I didn't think about forever in the beginning. Along with some friends (I need lots of moral support and accountability) I signed up for a twice-weekly yoga exercise class. It was more than uncomfortable at first. We were so weak in some areas that the poses were awkward and seemed nearly impossible. But we trusted that the teacher knew what she was doing. She had made a commitment to us and we to her. So we kept showing up, trusting, and trying.

Now, three years of exercise classes down the road, I look much the same to the observer. However, I feel a subtle but profound difference. The really dramatic change is that when I go to do something physical—to call upon these muscles in an out-of-the-ordinary way—they respond! They're not what I would like them to be and am continuing to work toward, but they're better than they were.

Let's make the switch now to our core spiritual muscles. It's a metaphor that works. Could we think of those muscles as being synonymous with our core Truths—Truths with a capital *T?* Could it be that if our core spiritual muscles are out of shape and flabby, we end up trying to do our work with lies and half-truths? And while those might be sufficient in everyday situations, when there is an extraordinary need they just aren't up to the job. When things like divorce, death, tragedies with children, financial calamities, and a multitude of extraordinary stresses cross our paths, we might reach for spiritual muscles, only to find that they simply aren't strong enough to catch us and give us the strength to lift our burdens. Then our conclusion might be that God doesn't care, and we might even turn our backs on Him and His Church. It has happened before and it could happen again—to you or to me—if we go along ignoring the simple, everyday training schedule for our spirits.

⌘

Would you turn back to your original list—the "I believes" that you put in place in chapter 3?

I am assuming that there is one particular belief that we have all written down in some form or another. Even the youngest Primary child can recite it. However, I believe there is some question about how flabby or how strong this belief really is when we put it amongst all the other half-truths and not-true-at-alls that flourish in our Belief Boxes. Here is how that belief looks for me:

TRUTH: I believe that I am a child of God—that I am His spirit daughter, precious in His sight, known completely, and loved beyond human comprehension.

President Gordon B. Hinckley elucidated this thought: "I believe in myself. I do not mean to say this with egotism. . . . I believe that I am a child of God, endowed with a divine birthright. I believe that there is something of divinity within me and within each of you" ("I Believe," 6).

Now, keep in mind our map.

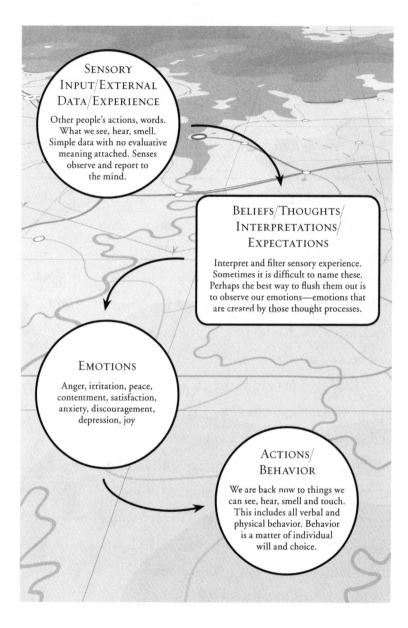

SENSORY
INPUT/EXTERNAL
DATA/EXPERIENCE

Other people's actions, words.
What we see, hear, smell.
Simple data with no evaluative
meaning attached. Senses
observe and report to
the mind.

BELIEFS/THOUGHTS/
INTERPRETATIONS/
EXPECTATIONS

Interpret and filter sensory experience.
Sometimes it is difficult to name these.
Perhaps the best way to flush them out is
to observe our emotions—emotions that
are created by those thought processes.

EMOTIONS

Anger, irritation, peace,
contentment, satisfaction,
anxiety, discouragement,
depression, joy

ACTIONS/
BEHAVIOR

We are back now to things we
can see, hear, smell and touch.
This includes all verbal and
physical behavior. Behavior
is a matter of individual
will and choice.

We are looking for experience—spiritual experiences that will confirm beliefs or thoughts that are True.

Perhaps this is easier to illustrate with a story. I am quoting from a talk given by Barbara Lockhart at BYU Women's Conference in 2006.

> When I was in my twenties, I skated in several Olympic Games as a speed skater for the United States. At that time, I thought my value came from my accomplishments. When I achieved a great deal and nothing changed within me, I was really confused. I loved what I could do but didn't really like myself. And no amount of success changed my negative self-talk and self-contempt. I had so much to hide. I felt that if anyone were to really get to know me, they wouldn't like me.

Now, it's very important for you to know something about my friend Barbara. She had already joined the Church when she talked about this feeling of self-contempt. She had already received a testimony of Joseph Smith and the restored gospel and had acted on that testimony by being baptized a member of The Church of Jesus Christ of Latter-day Saints. But she was still operating out of beliefs that were not true—beliefs that were creating negative emotions.

Did you hear her say that she *thought* her value came from her accomplishments? Did you recognize that bit of not-true-at-all she was carrying around in her Belief Box—thoughts that were creating subsequent negative emotions?

You see that she has two things she can do with this. First, she can confront the evidence for those beliefs, as we did in the previous chapters. Then she can identify the Truth—the real TRUTH that doesn't match the negative beliefs—and go about nourishing it, making it so healthy and strong and real that there simply is no dark corner in her Belief Box for those thoughts of worthlessness to grow.

She continues:

> It was only when I pled with Heavenly Father in a most fervent prayer to know if He loved me that my heart was changed. And that change didn't come immediately. I knew He loved me; He told me so. He gave me a powerful answer to my most earnest prayer, "Of course I love you. You are my daughter." But my negative self-talk had become so habitual that even though I knew He loved me, I still could

not bring myself to feel love for myself. I couldn't stand the disparity, the darkness, the loneliness I felt inside. With faith in God that He could change me, I pled with Heavenly Father night and day for some six months, and He eventually changed my heart ("Gift of Worth").

Perhaps now is a good time to mention that in the language of the scriptures, we often speak of a "change of heart." I believe that when we overlay the scriptures onto our model, we are talking about the Belief Box as being *both* our minds and our hearts. Beliefs aren't simply intellectual decisions, are they? They become beliefs when these thoughts go down into our very hearts. Remember that we said that our thoughts and beliefs come as a result of interpreting the sensory data coming in—and that sensory data includes spiritual sensory data, the experiences we have with the Holy Ghost.

Please reread that last paragraph from Barbara, because it says some important things about getting rid of untruths.

In our vernacular, Barbara—with the help of her Heavenly Father—did a little sorting and discarding. Her belief about her own worth—that it was based on her accomplishments—

was dismissed. And it was replaced with the Truth that God loves her. Did you notice how that happened?

In the next chapter, we'll talk about some possibilities for creating experiences that will give birth to and feed Truth—things as they *really* are.

Chapter Nine

STEPS TO FINDING
AND FEEDING TRUTH

But if ye will turn to the Lord with full purpose of heart,
and put your trust in him, and serve him with all diligence of
mind, if ye do this, he will, according to his own will
and pleasure, deliver you out of bondage.

MOSIAH 7:33

Now we begin the exciting process of finding and feeding
Truth. Truth delivers us from the bondage of half-truths
and lies. In very real ways, those erroneous or limiting beliefs
hold us captive and keep us from developing into our best
selves, individuals full of light and truth. We have come to
understand how we may have integrated erroneous beliefs into
our hearts and minds through sensory experience and data.

Now let's discuss some things we can do to invite and nourish eternal Truth.

EXERCISE FAITH

Faith is the leap, the decision we make, using our agency, that God *will* give us what He said He will give us. We do all of the other things that are discussed in this chapter because we believe He is there. Our faith unlocks His ability to speak to us. Our faith is embodied in our willingness to make and keep our covenants. Faith is where my friend Barbara started. Her faith was demonstrated as she was baptized. It was faith that took her to her knees to plead for confirmation about the truth that she is a daughter of God.

I have said that faith is a decision we make. I believe that. How do we indicate that we have decided to have faith? By keeping our covenants, certainly. And then what happens as we keep our covenants? As Elder D. Todd Christofferson taught us, "They [our covenants] *produce the faith* necessary to persevere and to do all things that are expedient in the Lord" ("Power of Covenants," 21; emphasis added).

I also believe that faith is, after all, a gift from God. It's not something we can completely earn on our own. So our choosing accompanied by His gifting becomes an upward widening spiral of growing faith.

Faith is the first principle of the gospel of Jesus Christ—so important and complex that it is beyond our understanding, but at the same time so simple that each of us can base our lives on it without knowing exactly how it works. We are told that some of us have the gift of faith and some have the gift to believe on the words of others. It matters not. We simply must choose to go forward in faith if we want to create experiences that will nourish Truth in our hearts and minds.

In our training of core spiritual muscles we could perhaps compare faith to the importance of breathing properly when we begin a yoga practice. Faith is a constant underlying fundamental of every spiritual exercise, just as proper breathing is for every yoga pose.

> *The process of identifying truth sometimes necessitates enormous effort coupled with profound faith in our Father and His glorified Son. God intended that it be so to forge your character.*
>
> ELDER RICHARD G. SCOTT, "TRUTH," 92

My exercise teacher started small, asking us just to show up and go a teeny bit beyond what we had been doing. She calls it working to the "edge of sensation." It's not pain, it's not exhaustion—but almost. It's just a little bit more than we are used to. And it requires a daily decision on our part to keep at it.

Solving daily problems by relying on Truth is a helpful way to slowly build spiritual strength. As we confront the daily difficulties of life—some bigger than others—we are pushed to "the edge of sensation" in exercising those spiritual muscles. We find out what soul-searching prayer is all about, what treasures the scriptures hold, what strength temple worship provides, and through it all how instructive, directive, and confirming the Holy Ghost is.

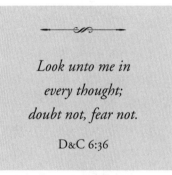

Look unto me in every thought; doubt not, fear not.

D&C 6:36

When the adversities are huge, we're no longer in training, but are at the point where we need to call on everything we have developed over time. And we can trust that it will be enough if we have paid the price.

PRAY

Of course, you noticed that as Barbara sought to fill her Belief Box with Truth—the Truth that she is a beloved daughter of God—she went directly to Him.

As we choose faith, we pray. Prayer is perhaps the most concrete and simple sign of faith. It is a child going to a Father. It is fundamental to receiving sensory data to feed core Truths. He has given us this wondrous gift—an invitation to pour out our hearts to Him. And with that invitation comes the promise that He will answer our pleadings. "If any of you lack wisdom, let him ask of God, that giveth to all men liberally, and upbraideth not; and it shall be given him" (James 1:5).

The scriptures are replete with assurances that the Lord will hear our prayers. None is more beautiful to me than this one from Isaiah: "He will be very gracious unto thee at the voice of thy cry; when he shall hear it, he will answer thee" (Isaiah 30:19).

> *The best way of finding truth is simply to go to the origin of all truth and ask or respond to inspiration.*
>
> Elder Richard G. Scott, "Truth," 90.

Sincere and effective prayers come from the desires of our souls—we want to pray. "With my soul have I desired thee in the night; yea, with my spirit within me will I seek thee early" (Isaiah 26:9).

Think of prayer as a fundamental exercise we use to build core spiritual strength. Like exercise for our bodies, it has to be consistent—every single day—to build strength.

Our part in prayer is to ask in faith—to ask to know the truth of specific things. His part is to answer in His own way and time. Did you notice that Barbara prayed for six months before she received her answer? And answers can come in many, many ways: the still small voice, the voice of someone else with a feeling of confirmation from the Holy Ghost, a passage of scripture, a lesson in Relief Society, a line from someone's testimony in fast meeting, a sentence from an article in the *Ensign*.

These answers are all delivered via the Holy Ghost. He is the instrument of reality, the testifier of Truth. "For the Spirit speaketh the *truth* and lieth not. Wherefore, it speaketh of things as they really are, and of things as they really will be" (Jacob 4:13; emphasis added).

So, now we are talking, really, about how to increase our opportunities to have experiences with the Holy Ghost, to create data that will help Truth grow continually stronger in our Belief Boxes.

Sister Julie B. Beck, Relief Society general president, has said, "The ability to qualify for, receive, and act on personal revelation is the single most important skill that can be acquired in this life" ("And upon the Handmaids," 11). I think it is interesting that Sister Beck refers to the receiving of personal revelation (is not that simply having the Holy Ghost operating in our lives?) as a "skill." A skill is something we practice, something we can become increasingly good at.

READ SCRIPTURES

Truth seems to simply seep into our bones as we read the scriptures. It's like the repeated dipping of homemade candles in hot wax. The accumulation is almost imperceptible, each layer of wax is so thin, but as you do it over and over and over, a candle grows beneath your very eyes. So it is with Truth. Remember, again, we are looking for experiences—experiences with the Holy Ghost. And the Spirit is simply in those pages.

Would you take one moment to think back on a time when you have received the Holy Ghost as you read the scriptures? You probably won't have to think back very far—probably this morning, as a verse caught your eye and you reached for a red pencil. That settled, good feeling we have when we pick up our scriptures and spend time in them is actually the presence of the Spirit. The scriptures are one of the surefire places we go to have experiences with the Savior and His teachings. That's what we want as we seek to exercise and build our core spiritual muscles. It's what our leaders want for us. It is, truly, our only hope for happiness and peace.

Scriptures help us to think clearly, to see things as they really are, to identify and nourish Truth. "We must allow scripture to stretch our reason back into shape. We must allow scripture to teach us how to think straight, because by ourselves we don't; we think bent, we think crooked. Gerard Manley Hopkins said, 'The Holy Spirit over the bent world broods with warm breast and with Ah! bright wings.' And the Spirit broods over us as we read this book, to straighten out our bent thinking; the world-views that have got twisted so that they are like the world's world-views. God wants us to be people, not puppets; to love him with our mind as well as our soul and our strength. And it is scripture that enables us to do that" (N.T. Wright, "How Can the Bible Be Authoritative?" para. 43).

> *My desire for you is to have more straightforward experience with the Savior's life and teachings . . . attention to the weightier matters of the kingdom, first and foremost of which is a personal spiritual relationship with Deity, including the Savior, whose kingdom this is.*
>
> Elder Jeffrey R. Holland, "'Come unto Me,'" 16

The scriptures contain the truths that God wants us to remember. They actually enlarge our memory by giving us the life experience of people throughout the ages. When we view their cultures and their individual lives at a distance we can clearly see patterns—those to avoid and those to embrace. For instance, Alma and Amulek encounter Zeezrom, who is teaching lies and half-truths. In a stirring story, he comes to see the damage that he has done, repents, and goes forward in teaching truth. I find the scriptural words interesting: "Zeezrom was astonished at the words which had been spoken [by Alma and Amulek]; and he also knew concerning the *blindness of the minds,* which he had caused among the people by his *lying words*" (Alma 14:6; emphasis added).

We see in this story how our minds can indeed be blinded by taking in lies. When Zeezrom tries to tell the people differently, they won't listen to him. They have become very adept at filtering out anything that might conflict with the beliefs they already hold. This is dangerous business, a high-stakes game for our salvation.

Another word for Truth is *doctrine.* We are beginning to see what President Boyd K. Packer meant when he said, "True doctrine, understood, changes attitudes and behavior. The study of the doctrines of the gospel will improve behavior quicker than a study of behavior will improve behavior" (*Mine Errand,* 307). If we place this sentence onto our road map, we see that encouraging true doctrine to enter our Belief Box will result in positive emotions and attitudes—peace, joy, happiness—which emotions in turn will change our behavior.

Truth and *righteousness* are two words that are often seen together in the scriptures. To me, *Truth* refers to what inhabits our Belief Box and *righteousness* is our behavior that grows out of truth—our covenant-keeping discipleship. They are intrinsically connected to each other.

FOLLOW THE LIVING PROPHETS

What do living prophets teach us at general conferences and other meetings? They teach Truth. And the Truths they teach are the ones that they know we are particularly in need of. How do they know? Because that is their prophetic gift. We open our hearts and minds in meekness and humility, and the Holy Ghost teaches and ratifies the Truth. He carries this spiritual sensory data into our hearts and minds to create ever stronger spiritual muscles.

If we want to feed the Truths and starve the lies, certainly we will take advantage of every opportunity to sit at the feet of prophets. We will treasure the general conference issue of the *Ensign,* study it, pray about it, absorb it. We will take advantage of podcasts, BYUtv, CDs, and DVDs that fill our minds with the counsel of prophets, seers, and revelators.

Sheri Dew recently told the following story:

Before each general conference I try to prepare myself spiritually so that I'll hear whatever the Lord wants me to hear and apply it to my life in the way the Lord wants me to apply it. Several conferences ago, during the first session, I had a very clear impression: "Sheri, you have the TV on too much." I almost said right out loud, "You've got to be kidding me. That can't be *my* problem!" To tell the truth, it kind of bothered me. Now, the impression wasn't about watching the wrong things, but about frequency. So I started thinking about it. "You have the TV on too much." Because I live alone and am something of a news junkie, I began to think that maybe I did have the TV on more than I realized. So, by the end of conference, I had made a promise to the Lord that I would cut my TV time back dramatically, and I even promised Him a percentage.

Two nights later I was teaching an institute class. We were having a general conference review, and one of the young women raised her hand and said she had had a remarkable experience with conference and she attributed it to the fact that she had prepared differently. From the time of the conference six months previous she had read a conference talk every day. She had read every talk from the last conference and then had gone further back. She said it had made a huge difference in the way she had experienced *this* conference.

"Wow," I told my class, "I've never done that." I wondered how I could fit that into my life. Then I thought about the time in the morning when I had been listening to the TV news while I got ready for my day. I began going onto LDS.org on my computer and dialing into the conference talks. I found that I could listen to two or three talks in the time it took me to get ready in the morning. In six months' time I listened to all the talks from the previous conference, then went back to others. Well, the combination of turning off the TV and tuning into talks from general conference was another way of saying, "I'm tuning out the world some and starting out my day listening to prophets, seers, and revelators." I cannot even begin to tell you what the combination of those things has done for my life, for the presence of the Spirit in my home, and for the frame of mind with which I begin my work. It truly makes a difference, tuning out the world and tuning into the prophets (unpublished typescript in author's possession).

Temple Worship

Several years ago I went to the temple seeking a solution to a problem. As the endowment session went forward, I kept pulling my thoughts back to the problem but found that my mind continued to drift. Somehow I just couldn't keep it fastened on the purpose for which I had come to the temple. About three-fourths of the way through the session, I decided to quit perseverating and just relax and let the spirit of the temple seep into me, assuming that for whatever reason, the solution to the problem was not going to be revealed to me that day and I might as well enjoy being in the house of the Lord.

In this relaxed and open frame of mind, I heard a phrase that was familiar to me but startling in its clarity—standing out as if it were printed in bold typeface. I knew that I needed to act on it. It had nothing to do—or so I thought—with the problem at hand, but the direction was so clear that I returned home and began to think and read and ponder on it over the next several months. It wasn't until years later, looking back on the positive outcome, that I realized the seemingly unrelated message from the Holy Ghost had, indeed, been the solution to my problem!

> *Sometimes our minds are so beset with problems, and there are so many things clamoring for attention at once that we just cannot think clearly and see clearly. At the temple the dust of distraction seems to settle out, the fog and the haze seem to lift, and we can "see" things that we were not able to see before and find a way through our troubles that we had not previously known.*
>
> PRESIDENT BOYD K. PACKER,
> "HOLY TEMPLE," 36

The temple is a place of revelation. One of the things we know is that Satan and his lies are barred from the house of the Lord. It is a place where we literally shut out the world, along with its half-truths and lies. If they come in, it is because we have brought them with us. So, check them at the door of the temple and let the Lord know that you have come to learn and understand His Truths. And remember that the Lord likes to do His own teaching in His house.

President Gordon B. Hinckley said, "I am satisfied that every man or woman who goes to the temple in a spirit of sincerity and faith leaves the house of the Lord a better man or woman" ("Of Missions, Temples, and Stewardship," 53). Certainly, people filled with Truth are better versions of themselves than if they were filled with half-truths and lies.

Of course, the Holy Ghost can be with us in many places and at many times, but isn't it wonderful that the Lord has provided a geographic spot—an actual place we can go, a building with walls where we put away our telephones, computers, and watches, change our clothes, and open ourselves to Him and His light. The Spirit of the Lord distills upon our souls in these holy houses, truly the most sacred places on earth. A new perception comes into focus of who we are, of what this life is really about, of the opportunities of eternal life, and of our relationship with the Savior—in other words, of Truth.

Temple work . . . gives a wonderful opportunity for keeping alive our spiritual knowledge and strength. . . . The mighty perspective of eternity is unraveled before us in the holy temples; . . . the drama of eternal life is unfolded before us. Then I see more clearly my place amidst the things of the universe, my place among the purposes of God; I am better able to place myself where I belong, and I am better able to value and to weigh, to separate and to organize the common, ordinary duties of my life, so that the little things shall not oppress me or take away my vision of the greater things that God has given us.

ELDER JOHN A. WIDTSOE, IN
CONFERENCE REPORT, 97–98

PONDER AND REMEMBER

Not too many months ago, Elder M. Russell Ballard came to our stake conference. He voiced great concerns over the state of the world, especially Satan's influence, and then just the sheer busyness of our lives. He pled with us to make time to be quiet . . . to sit, even just to hold our scriptures, and think about our lives. The Holy Ghost speaks to us quietly.

I believe one of the unexpected gifts President Thomas S. Monson is giving to us as members of the Church is a call to slow down. When he speaks, he tells stories, giving us time to step into someone else's life. And they are usually stories about taking time for individuals, enjoying the simple luxury of quiet visits and conversations. As we listen to him speak, we can almost feel ourselves slowing down a bit—entering a world that isn't about lists or the clock but rather about listening and responding to the promptings of the Holy Ghost.

Pondering time allows us to cast our minds back on times the Lord has spoken peace to our hearts (see D&C 6:22–23). As we remember those times, we give the Holy Ghost an opportunity to repeat His witness to us—to take more spiritual sensory data into our Belief Boxes. Some people set aside a little quiet time on fast Sundays. Others find a quiet time on

Mondays. Perhaps it will be in the early morning when you walk or exercise. Just empty out some kind of space where you can meditate. Examine your heart, mind, and life. Ponder, search, question, inquire, evaluate.

Pondering time is a time to notice and remember the tender mercies our Father in Heaven is so generous in sending us—little messages that He knows us and loves us. It may be a friend calling just when you need something, your favorite hymn coming as a personal message to you, or hearing a particular phrase in a Relief Society lesson. These additional witnesses, tender mercies, are small spiritual experiences that help truth go down into our very bones.

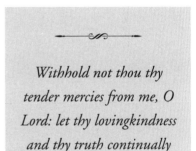

Withhold not thou thy tender mercies from me, O Lord: let thy lovingkindness and thy truth continually preserve me.

PSALM 40:11

The sacrament is all about remembering. *Remember* is a holy word because it points us to God's rescuing hand. It helps us emphasize Truth and it starves lies and half-truths. Those few minutes we spend every week thinking about the Savior will shape how we interpret the data coming into our Belief Box.

Covenants made, kept, and renewed weekly with the

sacrament give us the right to the continuing companionship of the Holy Ghost—the instrument and verifier of Truth. That is His promise—that we can have His Spirit to always be with us.

SPEAK TRUTH—OUT LOUD

Overlearn new thoughts, especially when modifying long-held habits of thinking. Say the correct belief 500 times. This may sound trivial, but it is perhaps one of the most simple and powerful tools we have.

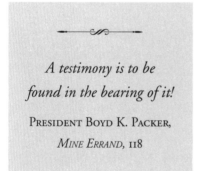

A testimony is to be found in the bearing of it!

PRESIDENT BOYD K. PACKER,
MINE ERRAND, 118

"Declare the things which ye have heard, and verily believe, and know to be true. Behold, this is the will of him who hath called you, your Redeemer, even Jesus Christ" (D&C 80:4–5). This is scriptural counsel given to missionaries, but I have no trouble applying it to each of us. We can speak out loud—even declare the truths we know. When we do so, the Holy Ghost witnesses anew.

This is one of the great blessings of participating in church—in classes as well as in the assignments and callings we have. They give us an opportunity to speak truth out loud.

S. Michael Wilcox describes his personal experience with teaching truth: "Sometimes I start a class or a talk feeling my soul is as empty as a dry lake bed and I have nothing to offer, but when I rise and begin to speak, the water of truth seeps in and fills me, and I know that I know. I am strengthened by my own voice. The memory of hearing the water flowing into me stays and sustains me even in the driest periods" (*What the Scriptures Teach,* 37).

LISTEN FOR TRUTH AND RESPOND TO IT

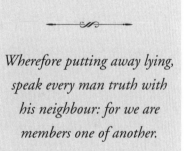

Wherefore putting away lying, speak every man truth with his neighbour: for we are members one of another.

EPHESIANS 4:25

My friend Madelyn teaches preschool. She interacts with all kinds of parents—many of them with lifestyles and beliefs much different from hers. She is amazingly effective with them because she sees every one of them as embracing some Truth—maybe not all of the Truth as she understands it, but *no one* is completely devoid of Truth. She has said: "When engaging in conversation I always listen carefully for Truth. When I hear it, I respond to it. That's where we go to continue our conversation. This not only strengthens me, but builds wonderful bonds of understanding and respect." Shared Truth, indeed, knits our hearts together.

IN CONCLUSION: ADD TIME AND PERSEVERANCE

Keep it small.

Keep it simple.

Give it time.

An exercise program such as yoga is a slow process. It is slow by design. But, in order to secure the gains and add to them, you have to keep it up. And guess what, the more you do it, the more your desire to do it grows. It is the same with building core spiritual muscles. You may have a period of intense growth—perhaps some adversity that drives you to your knees and calls forth the blessings of heaven. But to secure those gains, we must continue to invite the Holy Ghost into our lives—daily.

Time and perseverance are necessary companions to faith, prayer, scripture reading, hearkening to the words of living prophets, temple worship, pondering, remembering, speaking truth out loud, and listening and responding to truth.

Scriptural terms for this concluding point are *patience, diligence,* and *long-suffering.* I like the interpretation of *long-suffering* that points to the word *suffer,* meaning "to allow." It makes sense to me that the Lord is asking us to allow time—to recognize that spiritual maturity is a long, slow process. In contrast, Lucifer's promises (which he doesn't have the power or the will to keep) usually include instant rewards.

As we persevere in our efforts to find and feed Truth, over time we will become the people we were meant to be.

Chapter Ten

TRUTH MATTERS

And ye shall know the truth,
and the truth shall make you free.

JOHN 8:32

What is it like to live our lives out of truth, rather than out of distorted truth or lies? The first thing we will notice is a difference in our emotions. And after that, with no difficulty at all, there will be a change in our behavior; we will be able to do things that would not have been possible before.

Many years ago, as a relatively inexperienced member of the Primary general board, I was assigned to do some auxiliary training with Michaelene Grassli, the Primary general president, in a third-world country. It was a new and intimidating assignment and I was obviously concerned about being able to do my part well. At one point early in the week, we were with one of the local leaders. She was so excited to have us there and expressed it by telling us what a boost the auxiliary leaders who had come the year before had given the women leaders in her area. In fact, she went on and on in great detail about the amazing interactions and the lasting impact those visitors had had on the local members. And then she enthusiastically expressed that she *knew* we would do the same!

She showed us and our suitcases to a bedroom and closed the door. I was too tired even to cry, but in what seemed like an uncontrolled torrent of words I told Sister Grassli how inadequate I felt and how sorry I was that I was going to let her and the whole Church down by being less than what this woman expected.

Can you hear some untruths operating here? Certainly one of them is that I am supposed to have the same gifts and talents as other people in my situation have. Another might be that another person's strength or success somehow diminishes me—that it's a competition. And we would undoubtedly find more if we continued to clean out this closet. As with Charlie Brown, it could take more than one night!

But on with the story, because what Sister Grassli said changed my emotions almost immediately. She spoke Truth. She said, "Virginia, don't worry about what the others have done. All you have to worry about is pleasing Heavenly Father." There was an immediate emotional response from me as I took that Truth in and allowed it to resonate in my mind and heart. My emotions of anxiety and discouragement were replaced with peace. And my actions, I believe, reflected that confidence.

I find it curious that knowing we are accountable to God is less intimidating than thinking we are accountable to people we will probably never even see again! But that is the way of Truth. It fills us with hope, energy, and righteous desires rather than a sense of competition and inadequacy.

This is how Barbara, our speed skater, described her emotions and behavior when she prayed to have the Lord teach her the Truth that she was His daughter.

> The change was that I sincerely felt a tremendous gratitude for my life—grateful to be me. I honestly had never remembered feeling that I liked me, that I liked who I was. This newfound respect for myself enabled me to see myself as distinct from my behavior and my circumstances. The darkness, the negativism, the self-abasement was gone for good. He totally changed my life. No longer was I

emotionally needy, no longer worried about myself, that I was never good enough, obsessed with getting others' approval. Instead of being so self-absorbed, I became secure in my divine reality, that I am God's child, that He loves me, that I am precious to Him. No trial, no rejection, no circumstance has ever caused me to doubt or question His acceptance of me. This is reality. Life now is filled with finding ways of giving rather than being obsessed with getting ("Gift of Worth").

Take a moment to write down one of your own experiences—a time when emotions of fear or discouragement were changed as you tapped into the Truths you know.

⚜

We can all profit by getting more sensitive to the emotions and actions that flow out of Truth. When we speak Truth, and when we act on Truth, confirmation by the Holy Ghost follows. This creates stronger and stronger core Truth muscles, which in turn help us recognize more spiritual data, and so on. Do you see how this works? It's like a flywheel on a machine. At first it turns only with effort, but at some point it catches on and creates its own momentum. Truth begets truth, joy begets joys, love begets love.

We may not be completely successful in throwing away erroneous beliefs gained during childhood. But the experiences that created them *can* be consecrated for the welfare of our souls as we turn to the Savior and His atoning sacrifice. They will no longer hold our emotions hostage; they can actually lead us to compassion and understanding.

I love the Saints of the Restoration and find their stories inspiring. Like you, I have often wondered how they did what they did. The writings of Eliza R. Snow have helped me understand what I have come to call the spirit of Nauvoo—a spirit of optimism and faith in the midst of personal privation and suffering.

May I take you to Nauvoo shortly after Joseph's martyrdom? It was a

---

The many misconceptions, wrong assumptions, false notions, downright lies and irrational fears need to be pulled to the surface and repaired. One can't eject all these errors, but they can in part be replaced with other information. The difficulty is that in the brain, the oldest information is the most permanent. A belief of 20 years is harder to root out than a new discovery. Still, when falsehoods or distorted thinking pop up from childhood, they need to be smothered with truth.

JOE CRAMER, M.D.,
"BRAIN NEEDS," A15

difficult time, full of perplexities and displacement. Eliza's plural marriage to Joseph Smith could not be acknowledged publicly, or even privately, except between the two of them. He was her prophet, her fountain of truth. He was her husband, "the choice of [her] heart, the crown of [her] life" (Snow, "Past and Present," 37). And now he was gone. Although she never spoke of her feelings concerning this time, it was reported by a friend that Eliza was "prostrated with grief." As she was fervently praying to die, Joseph came to her, telling her that she had yet a great mission to accomplish in carrying forward the work he had established, "that she must be of good courage and help to cheer, and lighten the burdens of others" (Jenson, *Latter-day Saint Biographical Encyclopedia,* 1:695). She determined to do just that, even as she surely struggled with the "lonely feeling" that would sometimes "steal over" her (Beecher, *Personal Writings,* 52).

Many months later, living in an attic room with a ceiling so low that she could almost reach the rafters as she lay in bed; with only a chair, a table, and a candle; no carpet on the bare floor, she learned of the death of her dear father.

This tiny attic room became the place where, in the midst of renewed mourning, she found solace, wholeness, and connection by relying on the strength of Truth that was burned into her heart and mind. It was here that she penned the lines that would become our beloved hymn "O My Father." Understanding the Truths that Joseph Smith taught, strengthening them through obedience and personal prayer and study, she was able to live out of them. She saw herself not as an abandoned woman in a frontier territory but rather as a child of heavenly parents, nurtured by their side before this life, doing a work they had given her to do now, and at length returning to live with them.

Eliza's example teaches me the power of Truth. Yes, she struggled with loneliness and sadness and the usual worries of earth life. We all do. But those emotions didn't debilitate her. They didn't keep her from learning, growing, contributing, and being filled with peace, joy, and happiness for the remaining forty-three years of her life.

Two years ago my husband was diagnosed with ALS, a terminal and untreatable disease. As time went by and he lost the ability to do independently many of the things he had always done, I found myself physically stretched. During those months and weeks I found it necessary to call on every muscle I had developed through daily exercise. As I leaned over his bed for much of the time in the last weeks of his life, I called on core muscles and, to my delight, found that they were there.

Of course, I wished that they were stronger, but they were sufficient. And beyond those muscles I was grateful for the gift of good health. It was indeed a gift, not something I could exactly earn, but something that for the time being the Lord had granted me.

Jim's illness and subsequent death also required us to call upon spiritual muscles. To our relief, they were there. Our family began to understand what day-after-day habits of recognizing and feeding Truth meant as we faced extraordinary challenges. And along with what we had put into place over many, many years was the recognition that God in His generosity had given us the gift of faith and His outstretched hand—unearned and beyond what we could have done for ourselves. His grace was and is sufficient.

Truth matters. Everything we can do to find, feed, and strengthen it is worth the effort. We *can* live without fear. We *can* feel peace, joy, and happiness. We *can* diminish the clutter of lies and half-truths. We *can* have clear minds that think straight. We *can* act with the power of Truth. The Lord will help us.

He said, "Whatsoever is more or less than [truth] is the spirit of that wicked one who was a liar from the beginning. The Spirit of truth is of God. I am the Spirit of truth, and John bore record of me, saying: He received a fulness of truth, yea, even of all truth" (D&C 93:25–26).

Truth is inseparable from God the Father and His Son Jesus Christ. Our Redeemer, our Savior, the author and finisher of our faith, Alpha and Omega, the beginning and the end, is the supreme embodiment of Truth. And when we fill our minds and hearts with Truth we will see everything and everyone differently, including ourselves. We will see clearly. We will see through His eyes.

For who hath known the mind of the Lord, that he may instruct him? But we have the mind of Christ.

1 CORINTHIANS 2:16

Sources

Ballard, M. Russell. "Becoming Self-Reliant—Spiritually and Physically." *Ensign,* March 2009.

Beck, Julie B. "And upon the Handmaids in Those Days Will I Pour Out My Spirit." *Ensign,* May 2010.

Beecher, Maureen Ursenbach, ed. *The Personal Writings of Eliza Roxcy Snow.* Logan, UT: Utah State University Press, 2000.

Christofferson, D. Todd. "The Power of Covenants." *Ensign,* May 2009.

Cramer, Joe, M.D. "Brain needs continual tender loving care to thrive." *Deseret News,* April 17, 2010, A15.

Dollahite, David C., ed. *Strengthening Our Families: An In-Depth Look at the Proclamation on the Family.* Salt Lake City: Deseret Book, 2000.

Hinckley, Gordon B. "I Believe." *Ensign,* August 1992.

———. "Of Missions, Temples, and Stewardship." *Ensign,* November 1995.

Holland, Jeffrey R. "'Come unto Me.'" *Ensign,* April 1998.

Hymns of The Church of Jesus Christ of Latter-day Saints. Salt Lake City: The Church of Jesus Christ of Latter-day Saints, 1985.

Jenson, Andrew. *Latter-day Saint Biographical Encyclopedia,* vol. 1. Salt Lake City: Andrew Jenson History Company, 1901.

Kimball, James N., and Kent Miles. *Mormon Women: Portraits and Conversations.* Salt Lake City: Handcart Books, 2009.

Lockhart, Barbara. "Gift of Worth: Acts of Worthiness." Accessed online at http://ce.byu.edu/cw/womensconference/archive/2006/pdf/Gift_of_Worth-BarbaraDayLockhart.pdf.

McConkie, Bruce R. *A New Witness for the Articles of Faith.* Salt Lake City: Deseret Book, 1985.

Nelson, Wendy Watson. *Change Your Questions, Change Your Life.* Salt Lake City: Deseret Book, 2009.

Oaks, Dallin H. *Pure in Heart.* Salt Lake City: Bookcraft, 1988.

Packer, Boyd K. "The Holy Temple." *Ensign,* February 1995.

———. *Mine Errand from the Lord.* Salt Lake City: Deseret Book, 2008.

Scott, Richard G. "Truth: The Foundation of Correct Decisions." *Ensign,* November 2007.

Snow, Eliza R. "Past and Present." *Woman's Exponent* 15 (August 1, 1886).

Widtsoe, John A. In Conference Report, April 1922, 97–98.

Wilcox, S. Michael. *What the Scriptures Teach Us about Raising a Child.* Salt Lake City: Deseret Book, 2009.

Wirthlin, Joseph B. "Concern for the One." *Ensign,* May 2008.

Wright, N. T. "How Can the Bible Be Authoritative?" Lecture published in Vox Evangelica, 1991, 21, 7–32. Accessed online at http://www.ntwrightpage.com/Wright_Bible_Authoritative .htm.

Wright, Richard. *Black Boy (American Hunger): A Record of Childhood and Youth.* New York: HarperCollins Perennial Classics, 1998.

INDEX